happiness is ...

# happiness is ...

### 500 ways to be in the moment

Lisa Swerling & Ralph Lazar

CHRONICLE BOOKS

SAN FRANCISCO

taking the road less traveled

reading a book that's set in
the place you're traveling

seeing someone cry from
really good news

catching a rainbow in a prism

folding warm laundry

7

going right back to sleep
after waking up in the
middle of the night

tuning out distractions

just sitting and thinking

when your dog
licks your ear

forgiving a friend

a good scalp massage

sketching in an
art gallery

giving a gift for no
reason in particular

walking in deep snow

filling and burying a time capsule

writing down daily intentions

making your own
delicious-smelling soaps

taking in the view
from a bridge

reading the newspaper
cover to cover

a child mumbling in
their sleep

cooking with love

refusing to let anyone
steal your joy

flannel pajamas on the first
cold night of the year

jumping on hotel beds

feeling the wind in your hair

the smell of spring

a windowsill of
beautiful succulents

the quiet calm of a bookshop

finding the perfect
marshmallow-roasting sticks

the smell of lavender

reliving childhood games

exploring
new places

writing a letter to
someone instead of
sending an e-mail

sleeping when the
baby sleeps

goofing around
with friends

feeling beautiful from within

having a good sigh
every now and then

overcoming fears

letting the emotions flow

sharing homegrown veggies

cleaning to calm your inner chaos

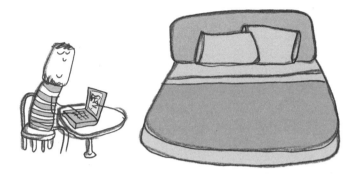

feeling inspired to write before going to bed

seeing the bulbs you planted in autumn
bloom in spring

sailing on a sunny day

being the bigger
person in a conflict

chasing a butterfly

31

*accepting the world as it is*

exchanging handwritten
letters with a friend

tidying your sock drawer

playing with little kids

the way the air feels
before a storm

perfecting the noble
art of having fun

a bubble bath on
a weeknight

helping someone
without being asked

alone time with a
notebook and pen

growing flowers in
the windowsill

dancing and singing at
the top of your lungs

taking a whole day for
an activity you love

a bunch of balloons

making an exceptional flower arrangement

thinking, dreaming, planning

a full moon hike

dreaming about the book
you're reading

wet, fresh-smelling hair

a small child
singing to you

41

a good stretch

spending a whole day
with your kids

going through a box of old
letters and photos

being yourself

running full speed into
the water

watching clouds

a good yoga class

taking the time to put
something together
properly

running your worries away

making an elaborate
sandcastle

a kiss on the forehead before bed

watching the rain slide off the roof

holding your mother's hand

painting a long wooden fence

finishing all your paperwork

losing track of time while
creating something

acting like children in public

climbing under
freshly cleaned sheets

a road trip with friends

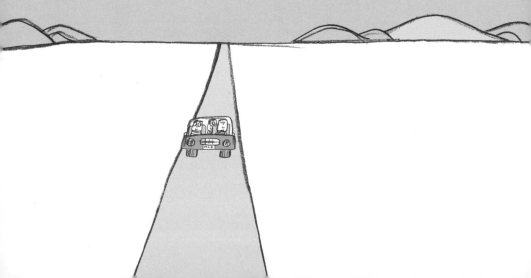

long talks with mom

scented candles

bouncy balls

fresh-cut flowers
at work

relishing
accomplishments

playing around
with someone
you love

feeling the rain on your face

not looking back

a cozy room with
twinkle lights

a perfect thinking spot

a glass of wine at the
end of a long day

drawing a perfectly
straight line without
a ruler

a no-boss-day
at work

having a friend who always
boosts your mood

a patch of wildflowers

hugging for no
reason at all

sitting back, relaxing,
and enjoying the flight

living within your means

a super productive
day at work

letting someone
spoil you

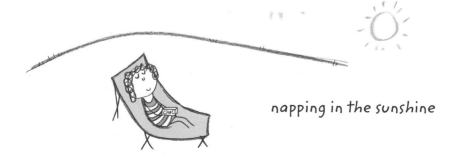

napping in the sunshine

waking up on a trip and
forgetting where you are

a wishing well

small gestures

a hot shower with the
perfect water pressure

walking on
crunchy leaves

when everyone appreciates
the food you cooked

spending quality time
with friends

watching a downpour

a summer water fight

lying on the sofa after a big meal

forgetting about the world
while playing your favorite
instrument

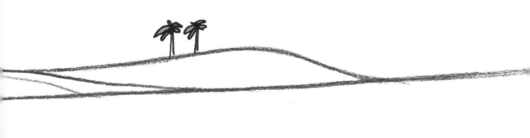

visiting your old school and
sharing memories

pausing for reflection

stopping by because you're
in the neighborhood

hugging good-bye but
not wanting to let go

coffee and a
long catch-up

staring out the back window

believing

72

knowing that better times lie ahead

sharing a hobby
with friends

decluttering

leaving money in the meter for the next person

seeing your dog after a long time away

getting new plants

when a butterfly
lands on you

enough coffee
for two

collecting firewood
on a beach

treating a friend to a meal

lending someone a book
you adored reading

the first sprouts of a new
garden

packing for an adventure

taking lunch away
from your desk

learning to read music

a bear hug from a child

being curious

saying sorry

letting go of things that make you feel bad,
and hanging on to those that make you feel good

deep conversations over dinner

admiring family photos

letting a child do your hair

being nice to people

a family art project

daydreaming

learning from life's teachers

poring over a map
to plan an adventure

finding the
perfect name for
your new blog

morning
meditation

a massage in a foreign land

writing a letter using
multicolored pens

decorating a birthday cake

hunting for shells

new frontiers

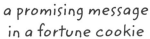
a promising message
in a fortune cookie

an outdoor shower

a big adventure

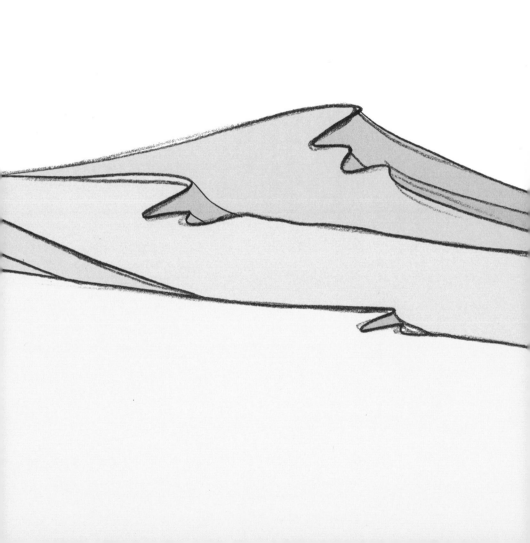

sweating out the stress

a kitty belly rub

hiding money in
someone's pocket

rewatching your favorite movie

the smell of your
mother's perfume

breaking the top of
a crème brûlée

a long beach walk

playing in the pool

planting a community garden

an empty laundry basket

finally playing a piece
of music correctly

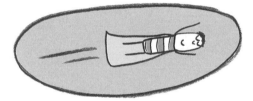

holding on to your dreams

jumping into a pile of leaves

finding a secret
place to write

having friends over to
your new apartment

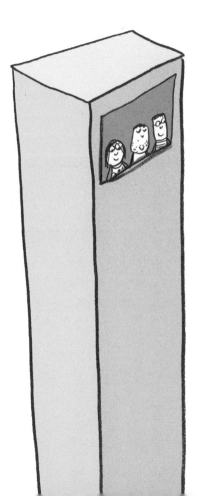

cheering
someone up

having a serious conversation in baby language

remembering all the words to an old song

giving the perfect gift

climbing your favorite tree

drawing with your feet in the sand

walking with a puppy

playing hide-and-seek

hiking with someone
small on your back

the first ladybug of spring

seeing an orchid
finally bloom

when for some reason
everything feels just right

traveling to a new country by yourself

celebrating your birthday with friends

dipping your nose into a bag of
freshly ground coffee

cooking a fancy meal for yourself

unpacking the last box in your new home

filling a whole journal

a smile creeping across
your face when a good
memory flutters by

waking up to find
your child has
climbed into your bed

dancing like the whole world has disappeared

going with the flow

taking
compliments
from a
stranger

the smell of a fire in the fireplace

sneaking outside to enjoy a morning cup of coffee

baking a surprise batch of cookies

making your own jewelry

writing the first line of
a new story

making pickles

asking an older person to
share stories from their youth

staying the course

your kids running to meet
you when you get home

designing your own house

making funny films
with friends

getting the slow-cooker
on in the early afternoon

shedding baggage and
traveling light

liking what you see
in the mirror

making a wish on
a dandelion

a spontaneous picnic

breathing deeply

not checking e-mail

savoring a perfect
macchiato

sitting outside on a warm night

writing a song for someone

embracing your
alter ego

starting a big project
with a friend

planning a surprise party

chilling out to
mellow music

unplugging from everything

accepting people
for who they are

having friends who know
what's important

finishing a drawing

expressing your unique sense of humor

taking a time-out

a yoga retreat

watching birds from your
window in the morning

exchanging smiles with an older
person on the street

feeling the sun
on your skin

coming home to the smell
of your favorite dish

homemade sodas

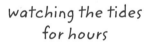

watching the tides
for hours

improvised games

having friends over to
watch an old movie

growing your own herbs
in the kitchen

exploring an old cellar

131

when you blow out the candles in one breath

making a dish from your
mother's favorite recipe book

letting your voice be heard

long stories from
little people

sunshine after
days of rain

arranging flowers you
picked from your garden

calling your dad
just to say hi

mastering a new skill

music that
perfectly describes
your mood

blending fresh juices

remembering that as one
door closes, another opens

goofing around with dad

trying your best
despite hardship

chatting with your neighbor

working as a team

a book that changes your life

giving a shoulder rub,
just because

being honest
with yourself

hot soup on a
chilly day

141

encouraging your
child's dreams

a sunrise excursion

dozing off while reading

not caring what others think of you

a free day with nothing to do

catching your
first wave

cooking dinner over the fire

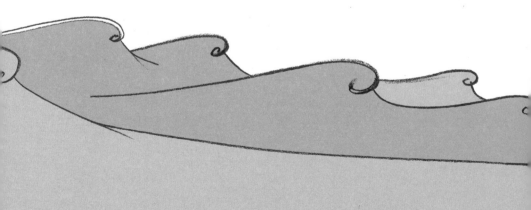

a girls' weekend

seeing the moon from your bed

writing something
you've already done on
your to-do list,
just to check it off

kissing often

cooking a huge gourmet meal

flying tiny paper
planes

a moment of inspiration

slowing down

someone apologizing before
you have a chance to ask

149

designing your own dress

your first handstand

making a giant salad and
your own dressing

fewer words,
more action

spotting a shooting star

a family dinner of
spaghetti and meatballs

fresh pajamas after a long bath

making time for coffee after lunch

playing a song
you wrote

being forgiving

a new haircut

the smell of
baby powder

letting your dog
hang out the car
window

writing a list of books you've
read in the last twelve months

*having friends who feed you*

sweeping the front
walk with a really
good new broom

a smile
with dimples

making a baby giggle

a bird feeder in the yard

blowing bubbles

coming home and
hopping straight into bed

walking barefoot
on wet grass

helping someone who is lost

making soup with vegetables
you grew yourself

driving less, cycling more

rearranging your bookshelf
in alphabetical order

the sense of being a kindred spirit with someone you've just met

sharing your last piece of chocolate

designing your own invitation

telling someone
they're appreciated

being a hero in little ways

standing below
a giant tree

sending a friend flowers
when they're down

when reality is better
than expectations

doing woodwork

capturing a small
moment on camera

listening to
solid practical advice

babysitting free for a friend

choosing your own path

a team huddle

laughing at old pictures
of each other

a well-deserved
vacation

grilling on a summer's day

a little alone time every day

leaving all your regrets behind

dancing to an old favorite tune

making snow angels

a comfortable silence

holding a gem to the sun

letting the waves tickle your toes

that first sip of champagne
on a special occasion

having a friend crash
on your couch

a whole day at the beach

drying clothes on the line

getting ready for a
dress-up party

wrapping yourself in a
fuzzy blanket straight
from the dryer

sitting on your surfboard
waiting for a wave

seeing big fish from the rocks

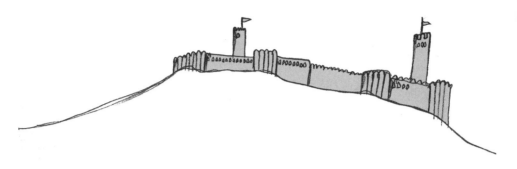

exploring a distant hilltop fort

knowing the owner of your local deli

creating your own language
while traveling

walking to work

an old-fashioned desk with
lots of secret drawers

a day at the spa

feeling the breeze

learning a poem
by heart

researching places for
an upcoming trip

water with
cucumber and
lemon

saving for a special day

finding a shelf of books in your
language in a foreign bookshop

cutting back on
caffeine

successfully squeezing
out that last teeny bit
of toothpaste

cracking a joke in a boring meeting

practicing yo-yo tricks

soaking in a hot spring

getting lost in a new city

coming home to a
tidy house

biting off the end of the
baguette on your way home

sneaking a note in the lunch box

making friends in the
pool on vacation

writing a bucket list

making up stories

the perfect workout
soundtrack

bugging someone when
they're on the phone

going for a walk
with no destination

learning to cook

watching a summer storm pass by

taking off wet shoes

sharing secrets

the reliable sound of
a grandfather clock

playing in waves

a solo hike

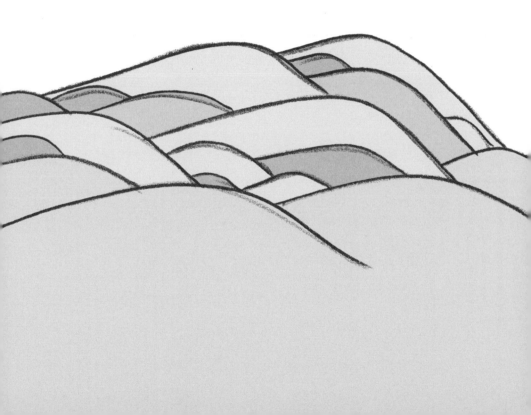

preparing for a big family visit

a horizontalish palm tree

a basketful of lovely new yarn

an indoor picnic

a rooftop terrace

greeting the sunrise

sampling at an
ice-cream shop

finding a beautiful
feather

the perfect
power nap

aromatherapy

noticing that your kids
have turned out to be
good people

rereading your
favorite book

a pickup game in the park

rolling down a sand dune after a swim

finding a water
fountain when you are
really thirsty

understanding directions given
in a foreign language

when a toddler's laugh
makes you laugh

catching your dinner
while camping

hosting a clothing swap

mowing the lawn on a beautiful day

when the paper is full of good news

running with dogs to the park

making someone laugh

landing in a new country

# finding your balance

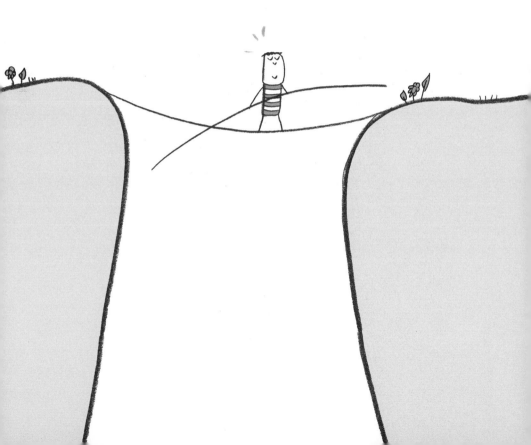

a collection of collections

a camping trip with friends

a hat with ears on it

a generous helping
when you're really
hungry

understanding the tides

playing Frisbee all afternoon

a long country drive

takeout on the sofa

being proud of yourself

meeting a friend for an impromptu lunch

just being together

weekend craft projects

feeling on top of everything

a backyard fire

being patient while standing in line

reading a book in the garden

a class photo you save forever

exchanging
friendship bracelets

getting out the muscle
knots during a massage

a hot tub in a
cold place

taking your time to
climb to the top

shouting YEE HAW!
just because

rocking a baby
to sleep

bringing food to a
needy person

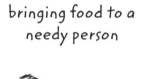 

making Popsicles on a hot day

calling your dog for dinner

cooking someone their favorite meal

silencing the inner editor

a picnic on the top of a
mountain

snuggling with a purring cat

dropping a letter
into the mailbox

releasing a paper lantern

touring a new place
with a superb guide

exploring the universe
through a telescope

a baby falling
asleep on you

dressing up for no reason

greeting strangers from
the bus window

experimenting in the kitchen

speaking a new language

sharing good news

freshly squeezed orange
juice

a bird eating from your hand

sweet solitude

getting something
exciting in the mail

rocking your bed head

YES!

saying yes

spending time in nature

an unexpected
phone call

visiting an ancient
place

making paper boats and floating them in a puddle

daydreaming through the commute

 teaching a
child to read

expressing
yourself

 sitting by a warm
heater on a cold
morning

visiting a natural wonder

playing a new favorite
track on repeat

a whole day spent gardening

watching the flames dance in a fire

racing to get back home

playing
make-believe

making someone smile
when they're sad

finding a four-leaf clover

a day out with a camera

opening a surprise

dropping everything for a chat

snuggling under the covers when it's cold

watching the sky from a hammock

a friendly feud

pulling a weed out by
its roots

finding your perfect match

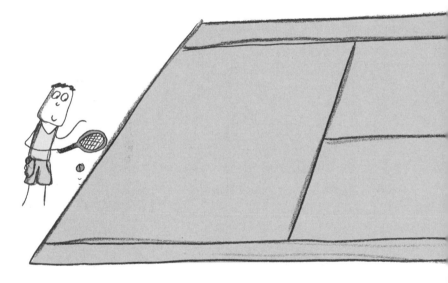

healthy competition

telling someone they inspire you

smiling at a
stranger

flipping a pancake

rubbing your friend's
pregnant belly

a lazy day with your
favorite person

253

turning
cartwheels

watching whales

cracking the ice
surface on a puddle

making footprints in fresh snow

slowly slurping a long noodle

watching wildlife

*complimenting someone's haircut*

a candlelit dinner

taking a kid for a shoulder ride

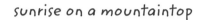

a morning swim

a close game
of cards

a big warm hug from a
treasured friend

doing your small part
to change the world

when water sparkles at sunset

a giggle fest

waking up to the sound of birds

going back to the house you grew up in

the sound of something
sizzling in the oven

washing your hair with
fabulous-smelling new
shampoo

guessing the number of grains
of sand on a beach

a night out at
the movies

the smell of chocolate chip
cookies fresh out of the oven

telling old family jokes

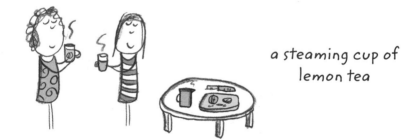

a steaming cup of
lemon tea

waking up to the sun
shining on your face

lying in the bath until
your fingers and toes
go all wrinkly

finding a whole
new perspective

reading late
into the night

appreciating
this moment

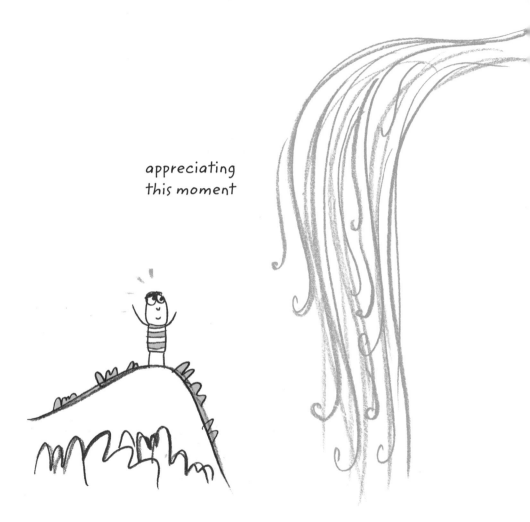

ISBN 978-1-4521-5201-1

Manufactured in China.

FSC
www.fsc.org
MIX
Paper from
responsible sources
FSC® C008047

Design by Lisa Swerling and Ralph Lazar

10 9 8 7 6 5 4 3 2 1

Chronicle Books LLC
680 Second Street
San Francisco, CA 94107
www.chroniclebooks.com